Coloring Diva's Mandalas

50 Mandalas with a Difference

Series 1

Tankard and Bax

ISBN-10: 8894122808
ISBN-13: 978-8894122800

Sign up for the Drama Llama Press newsletter to hear about our new releases and get our short problem solving e-book *Solved in a Day* free.

Click here to get started or go to www.dramallamapress/newsletter/

TO OUR MOTHERS

This book is dedicated to our wonderful mothers who inspired, encouraged and drove us to succeed in all things.

CONTENTS

Introduction 7

About the Authors 11

1. All Eyes on You! 13

2. Angry Cats 15

3. Art Deco Lighthouses 17

4. Bees on Steroids 19

5. Beetle Bums 21

6. Cacophony of Choir Boys 23

7. Camouflaged Leopards 25

8. Chinese Farmers on Pogo Sticks 27

9. Chinese Temples 29

10. Clashing Cymbals 31

11. Crazy Birds 33

12. Daft Dogs 35

13. Dancing Dung Beetles 37

14. Dazzling Pharaohs 39

15. Drawing Ducks 41

16. Eyes Round a Lily Pad 43

17. Fishy Tales 45

18. Gobsmacked Aliens 47

19. Gormless Babies 49

20. Howling Owls 51

21. Just Batty 53

22. Kamikaze Fish 55

23. Kings of The Deck 57

24. Masked Cats 59

25. Men in Black 61

26. Moths to a Flame 63

27. Off with their Heads! 65

28. On Cloud Nine 67

29. Owl Graduation 69

30. Papuan Huli Men 71

31. Parliament of Owls 73

32. Pincer Movement 75

33. Psychedelic Mushrooms 77

34. Ready for Take Off! 79

35. Rocket Launch 81

36. Rockin' Rockets 83

37. She Sells Sea Shells 85

38. Shy Rabbits 87

39. Sleeping Angels 89

40. Spotty Swallows 91

41. Surprise! 93

42. Talking Terriers 95

43. Technicolor Yawn 97

44. The Butterflies' Christmas 99

45. Tiger Divas 101

46. Tiger Lily 103

47. Toadstool Fairy Ring 105

48. Traumatized Tortoises 107

49. Tribal Trouble 109

50. Very Inca 111

INTRODUCTION

Why Coloring In for Adults?

In today's busy world, where we all seem to be juggling more things in the air than Coco the clown, it can be very difficult to chill out and switch off, although, God knows, we all try hard enough!

If you are like us, you will have attempted so-called "relaxing" activities to try to calm your turbulent brains, like watching (un)reality TV, eating a ton of chocolate or downing the week's wine ration in one evening. Does it work? Does it hell!

Stress is a cunning little minx. Just when you have made her walk the plank of the good ship Relaxation and kicked her to the ocean floor, up she bobs again to taunt you like a demented mermaid.

Fear not! There **is** a solution! A simple, enjoyable and effective way to calm yourself, relax and, as a bonus, come up with some brilliant creative ideas and solve some tricky problems as well. It's true! You *can* banish Mad Mermaid Mind to the seabed until you are ready for her again.

As you have already bought this book, you may have an inkling what this solution is. Yes... coloring in. We all had coloring books when we were kids, but coloring in for adults has taken off dramatically in the last year or so. Allowing your inner child to escape from your inner au pair for a while through the deceptively simple act of applying crayon to paper is so cool it's positively Arctic.

Coloring in is cheap, it's accessible, it's fun and it works. You don't need expensive equipment, a uniform, training or a gym membership. Just some crayons or felt pens and a coloring pattern book. Even better, it doesn't make you gain weight or give you a hangover. What's not to love?

The Science Bit

Oh, we all love a bit of science, don't we? It helps us justify our new found passion for coloring books to those responsible adults around us who may feel we have lost the plot. So here goes.

Our modern lifestyle often leaves us feeling stressed and anxious. When our wheels are spinning or we are engaged in the torture known as multi-tasking we are in a flight-or-fight state. This is a hangover from our cavemen ancestors, whose daily lives mostly comprised physical threats (sabre-tooth tigers, falling trees, rival cave people) demanding physical responses (fight, run). The reaction in the body to these dangers is to fiddle around (scientific term) with various chemicals and organ functions thus enabling us to either slay the tiger or run like hell. Once the danger is over then things reverse and we go back to making Tyrannosaurus soup or weaving a fetching loincloth.

That is fine if being chased by a tiger, not so good if you are hunched in an office chair or at the wheel of a car in a traffic jam. Many of our 21st century "threats" are not physical at all but our bodies still react as if they were, washing us full of chemicals like adrenaline, norepinephrine and cortisol, designed to help us move faster or hit harder. If we don't run madly through the office like a gazelle or hurl a wooden club at the boss then these chemicals stay in our bodies and end up making us feel like crap.

Ideally, when we are trying to relax, but not sleep or float away, we want our brains in an alpha state. This helps counteract the anxiety and stress and rebalance us. Coloring in, with its gentle, repetitive movements, clear simple focus, creativity, logic and association with childhood, helps move the busy beta brain into the agreeable, abstracted alpha state.

Some Helpful Hints

Coloring in is, quite literally, child's play, but in case you have forgotten then here are a few guidelines:

- There are no rules.

- Colored pencils are better than alcohol based liquid colors which bleed through.

- Try coloring in to background music. Whatever floats your boat. Baroque music (Bach, Mozart) is good to get you into that all-important alpha state of relaxation.

- Don't feel as if you have to complete a whole design in one sitting. You're not at the office now, you know. There are no deadlines.

- Buy a pencil sharpener alongside your colored pencils. You don't want to be stressed and stalking round the house looking for a bladed instrument to re-sharpen your blunt crayons.

- Keep an eye on how relaxed your body is. Do you really need to hold the pencil with a white-knuckle death grip? Are you coloring so hard you are leaving marks on all the pages underneath? Are your pencils snapping like matchsticks? Are you screaming at all? Those may be clues you are too tense! Consciously make yourself relax.

- Put a pad of paper or a magazine under the design if you are, despite our advice, using colors that may bleed through or if you are scribbling hard like a maniac, in which case, see above.

- If you have a problem to solve or decision to make, try thinking about it before and then after a coloring session. You may find the solution appears as if by magic.

- Coloring is a great sleep aid, so try a coloring session before bedtime to help you easily access the Land of Nod.

- Play around with different colors to see how they affect your mood. If you need to feel energized and revitalized, try reds, pinks and oranges. For a calmer vibe, try blues, greens and turquoises.

- Resist the urge to analyze what you have done. This is coloring. It's fun for its own sake. Remember fun?

- Enjoy yourself!

ABOUT THE AUTHORS

Fiona Tankard and Kathryn Bax are friends and recovering Type A personalities who are fibre artists both living in Tuscany, Italy. Their quest to calm down and chill out has led them to try a number of tools, including the wonderful world of adult coloring books.

They live 10 minutes from one another in the beautiful Casentino Valley, the "Hidden Tuscany" of thick chestnut forests, wild boar, deer on the doorstep and beautiful stone farmhouses and castles dotting the countryside. An area inhabited centuries ago by the Etruscans, it has inspired many artists throughout the ages, and was once home to Saint Francis and Michelangelo.

It is within these surroundings that Fiona Tankard and Kathryn Bax live, each keeping fiber animals to use for their weaving company. Fiona keeps alpacas, and Kathryn keeps Angora goats and Finnsheep. Both ladies are very creative, and love working with color and design.

A thing of beauty is a joy forever.

English proverb

1. ALL EYES ON YOU!

Memory is the treasure of the mind.

English proverb

2. ANGRY CATS

In the hour of adversity be not without hope, for crystal rain falls from black clouds.

Niẓāmī

3. ART DECO LIGHTHOUSES

*Human experience, like the stern-lights of a ship at sea,
illumines only the path which we have passed over.*

Coleridge

4. BEES ON STEROIDS

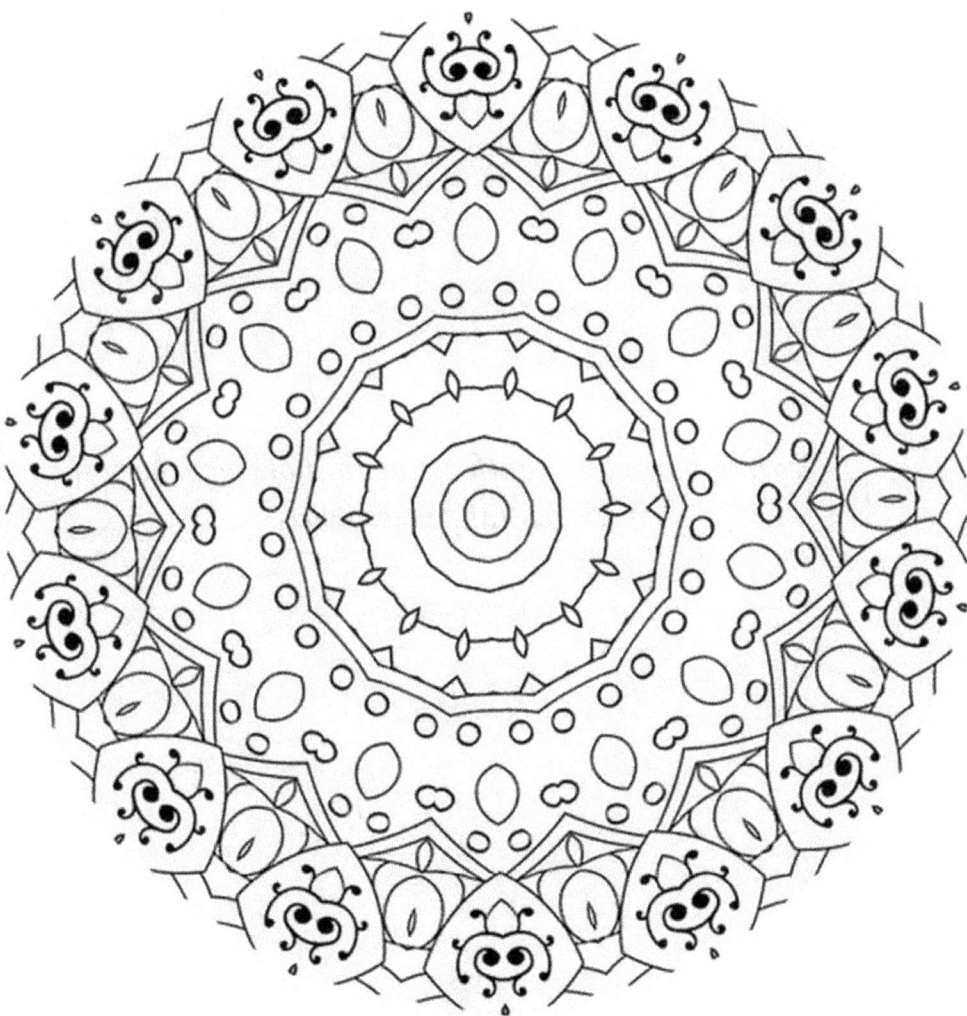

In learning, age and youth count for nothing: the best informed take precedence.

Chinese saying

5. BEETLE BUMS

We are never so much disposed to quarrel with others as when we are dissatisfied with ourselves.

Hazlitt

6. CACOPHONY OF CHOIR BOYS

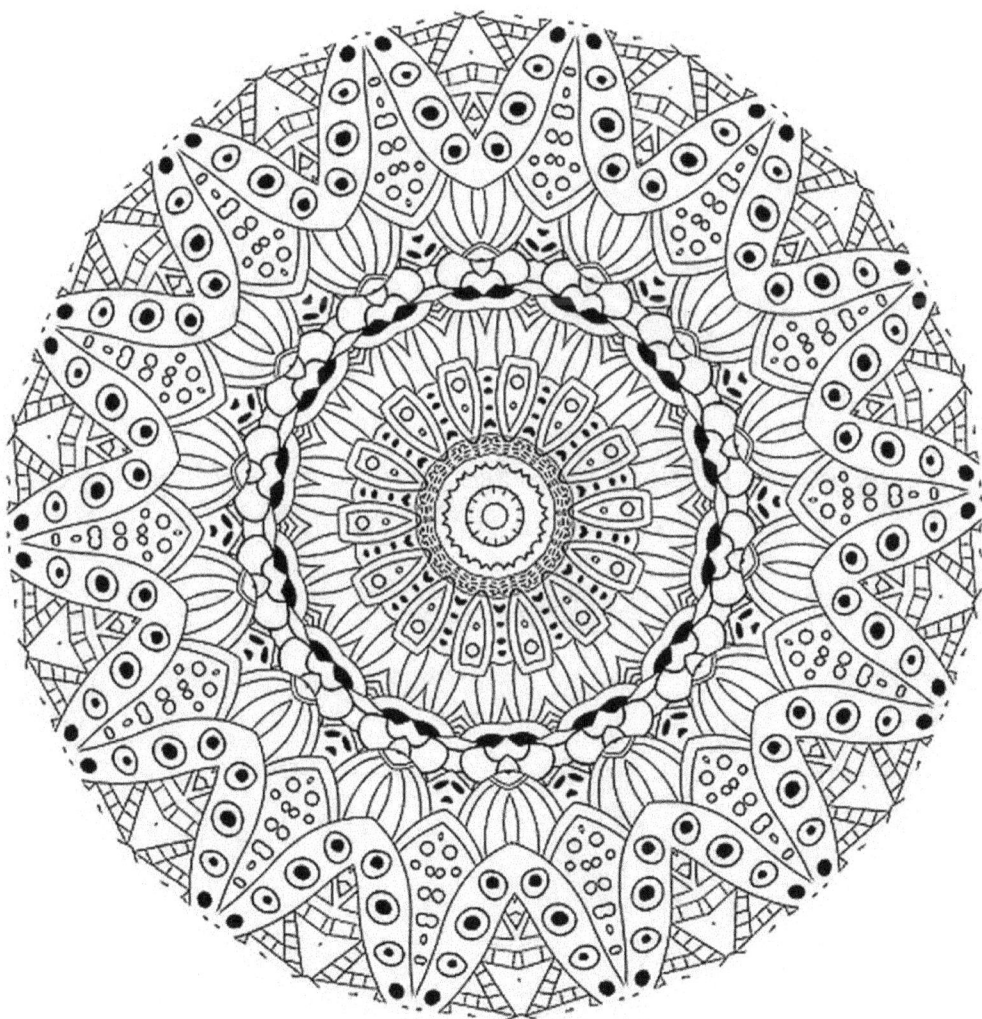

The gem cannot be polished without friction, nor man perfected without trials.

Chinese saying

7. CAMOUFLAGED LEOPARDS

The rays of happiness, like those of light, are colourless when unbroken.

Longfellow

8. CHINESE FARMERS ON POGO STICKS

Be not anxious about the trouble which is not yet come.

Firdausi

9. CHINESE TEMPLES

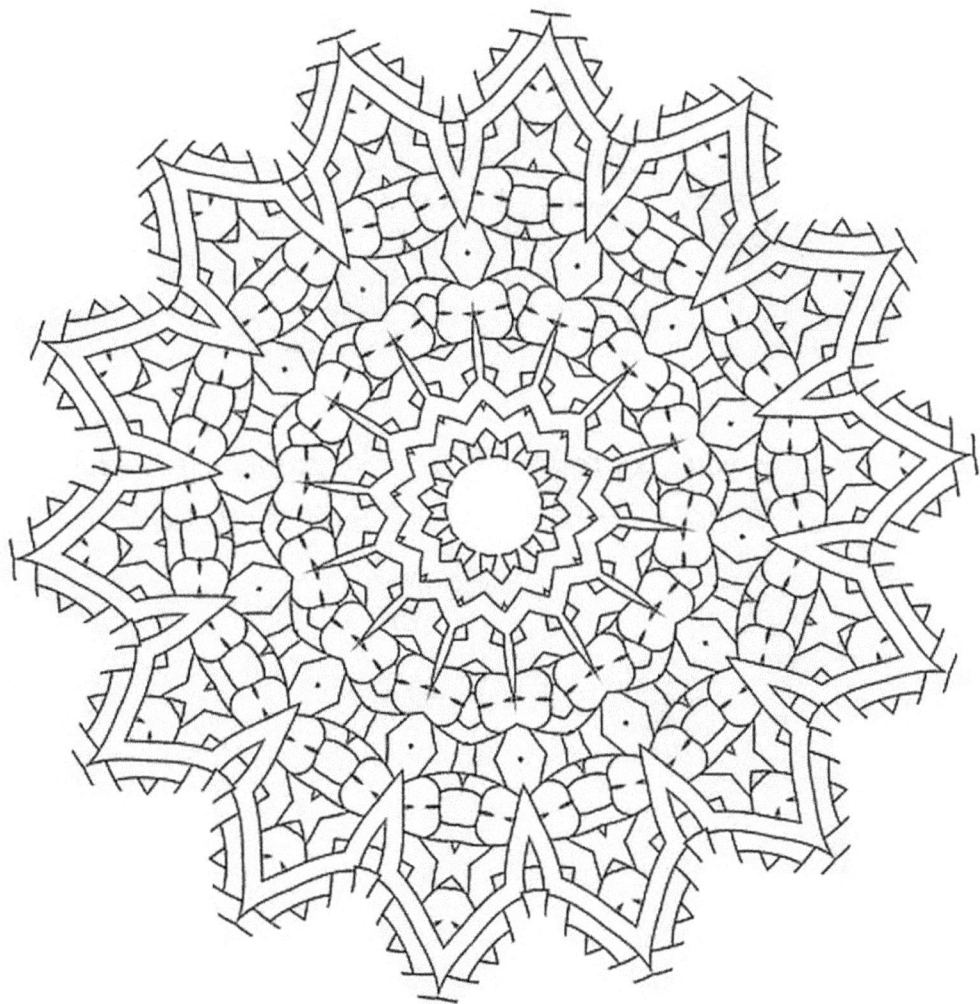

A wise man adapts himself to circumstances, as water shapes itself to the vessel that contains it.

Chinese saying

10. CLASHING CYMBALS

That energy which veils itself in mildness is most effective of its object.

Māgha

11. CRAZY BIRDS

People are not to be judged by their looks, habits, and appearances, but by the character of their lives and conversations.

Sir R. L'Estrange

12. DAFT DOGS

To exert power in doing good is our most glorious task.

Sophocles

13. DANCING DUNG BEETLES

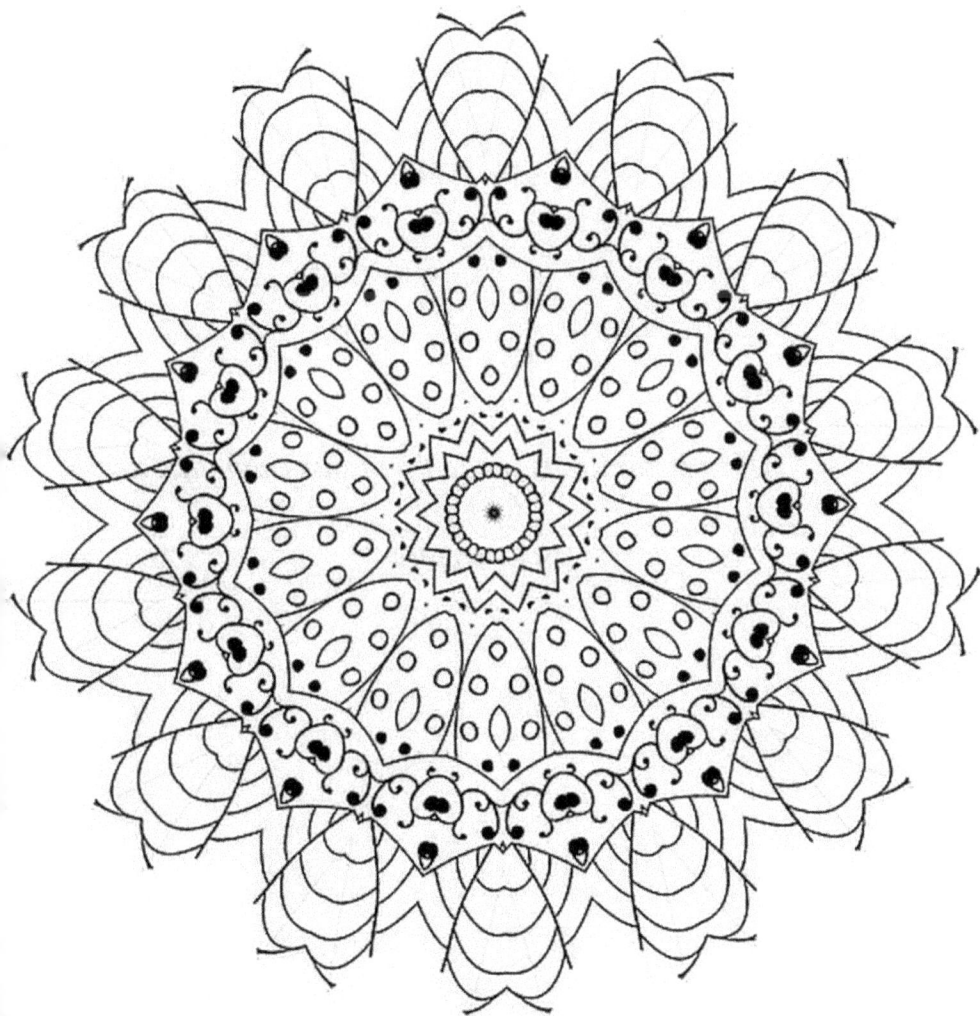

All that we are is made up of our thoughts.

Dhammapada

14. DAZZLING PHARAOHS

Depend not on another, rather lean upon yourself; trust to your own exertions.

Manu

15. DRAWING DUCKS

A wise man takes a step at a time; he establishes one foot before he takes up the other.

Sanskrit

16. EYES ROUND A LILY PAD

The first forty years of our life give the text, the next thirty furnish the commentary upon it.

Schopenhaue

17. FISHY TALES

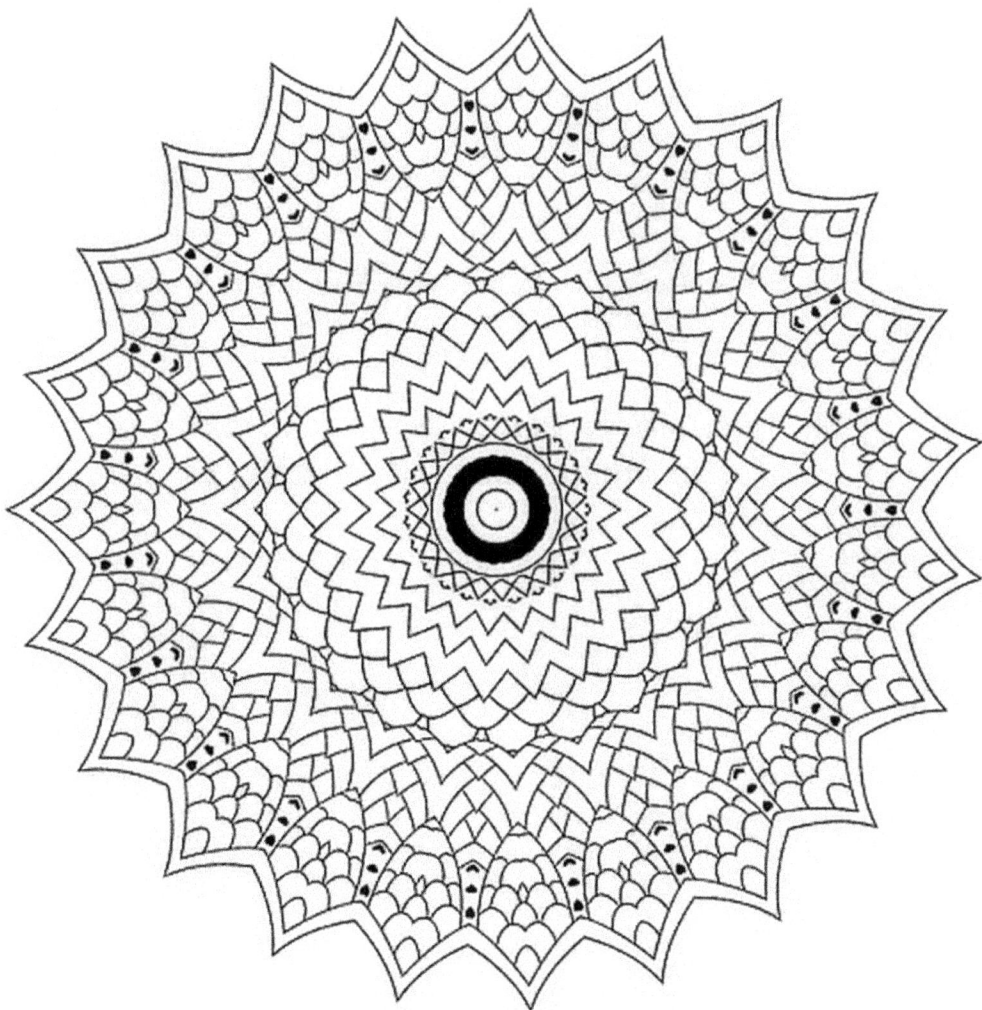

Never does someone portray their own character more vividly than in their manner of portraying another.

Richter

18. GOBSMACKED ALIENS

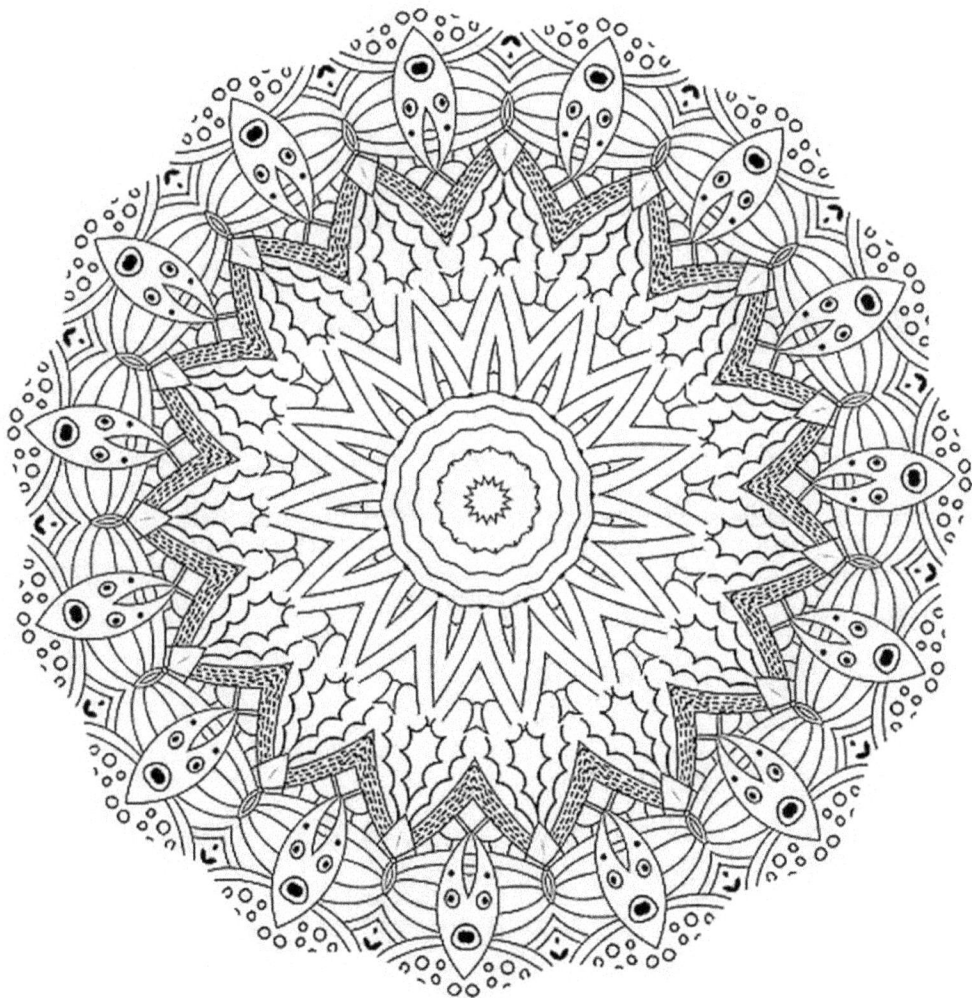

The woman who is resolved to be respected can make herself be so even amidst an army of soldiers.

Cervantes

19. GORMLESS BABIES

Everyone is the maker of their own fortune.

Anonymous

20. HOWLING OWLS

Be very circumspect in the choice of the company you keep.

Quarles

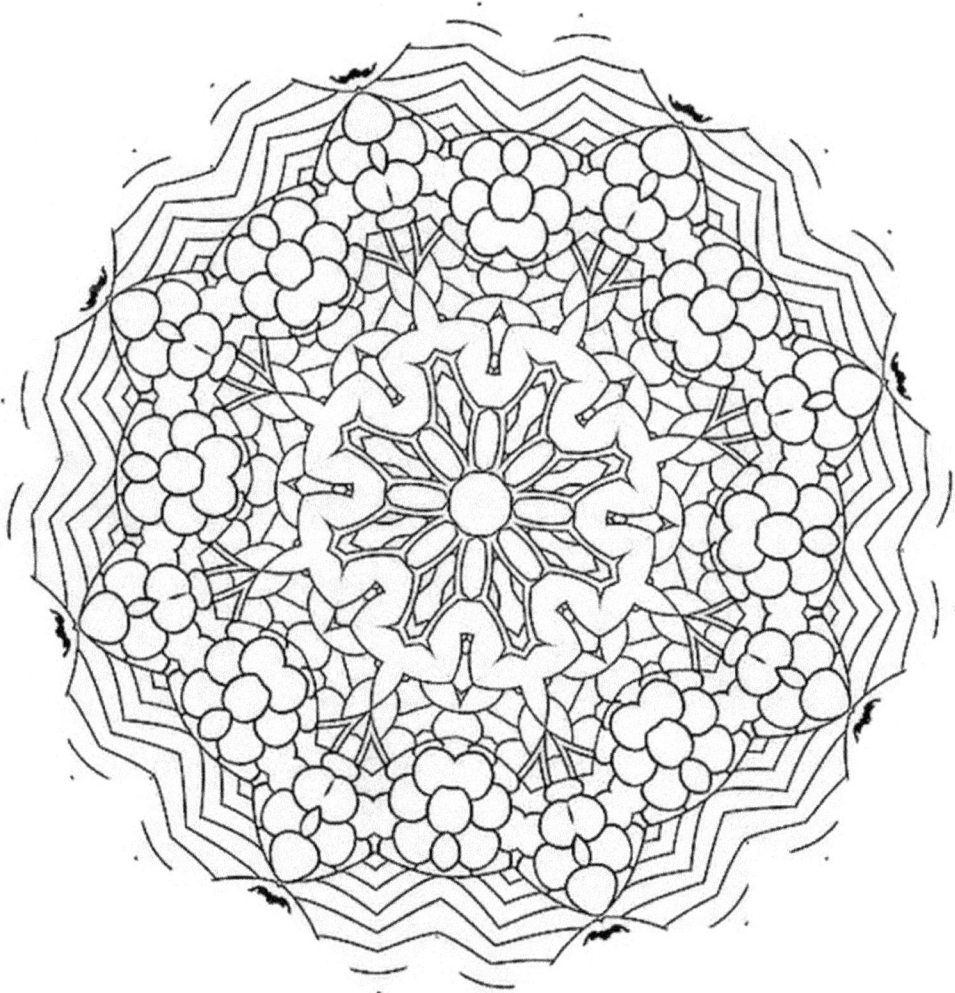

21. JUST BATTY

The person who talks much and never acts will not be held in reputation by anyone.

Firdausī

22. KAMIKAZE FISH

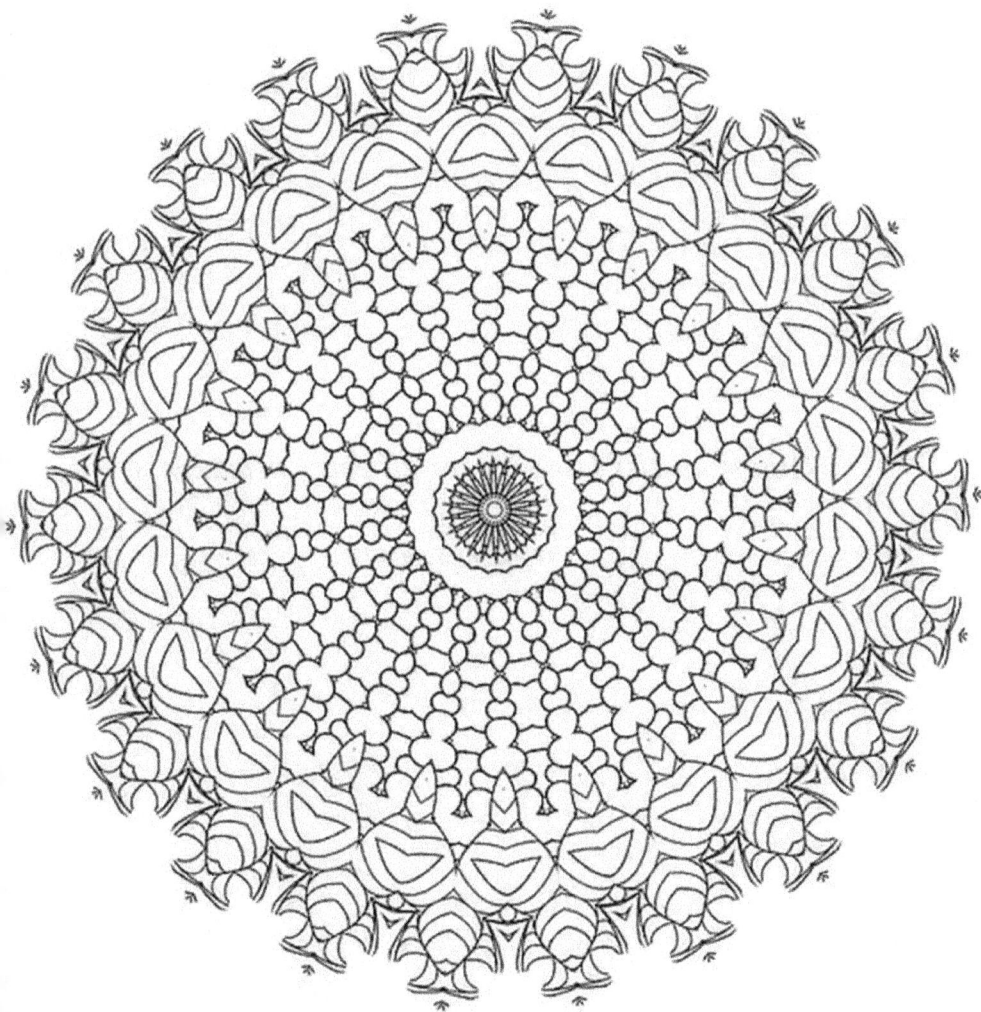

Opportunities lose not, for all delay is madness.

Turkish saying

23. KINGS OF THE DECK

Man is the only animal with the powers of laughter, a privilege which was not bestowed on him for nothing.

Egerton Smith

24. MASKED CATS

Amongst all possessions knowledge appears pre-eminent.

Hitopadesa

25. MEN IN BLACK

He is happiest, be he king or peasant, who finds peace in his home.

Goethe

26. MOTHS TO A FLAME

To form a judgment intuitively is the privilege of few.

Schopenhauer

27. OFF WITH THEIR HEADS!

How can we learn to know ourselves? By reflection, never, but by our actions.

Goethe

28. ON CLOUD NINE

We are more sociable and get on better with people by the heart than the intellect.

La Bruyère

29. OWL GRADUATION

Whoever brings cheerfulness to his work, and is ever active, dashes through the world's labours.

Tieck

30. PAPUAN HULI MEN

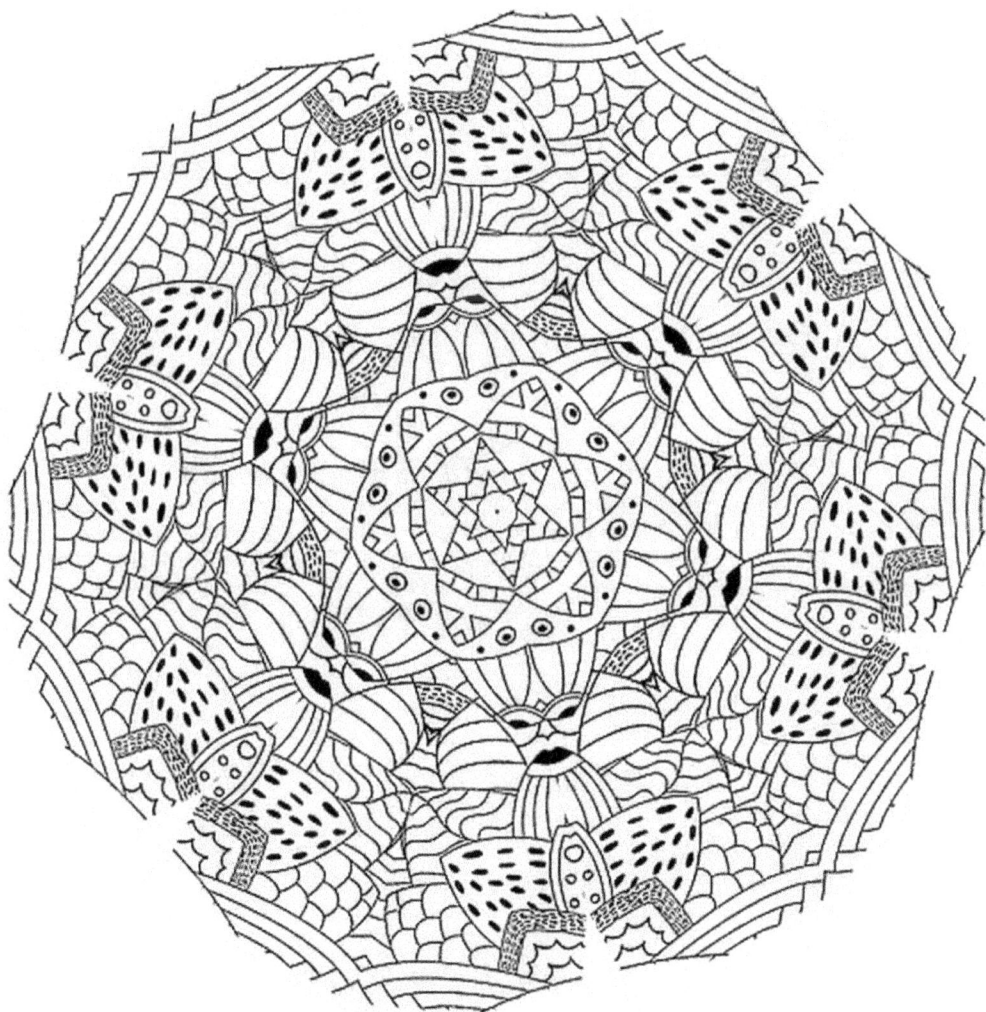

True happiness consists in making happy.

Bhāravi

31. PARLIAMENT OF OWLS

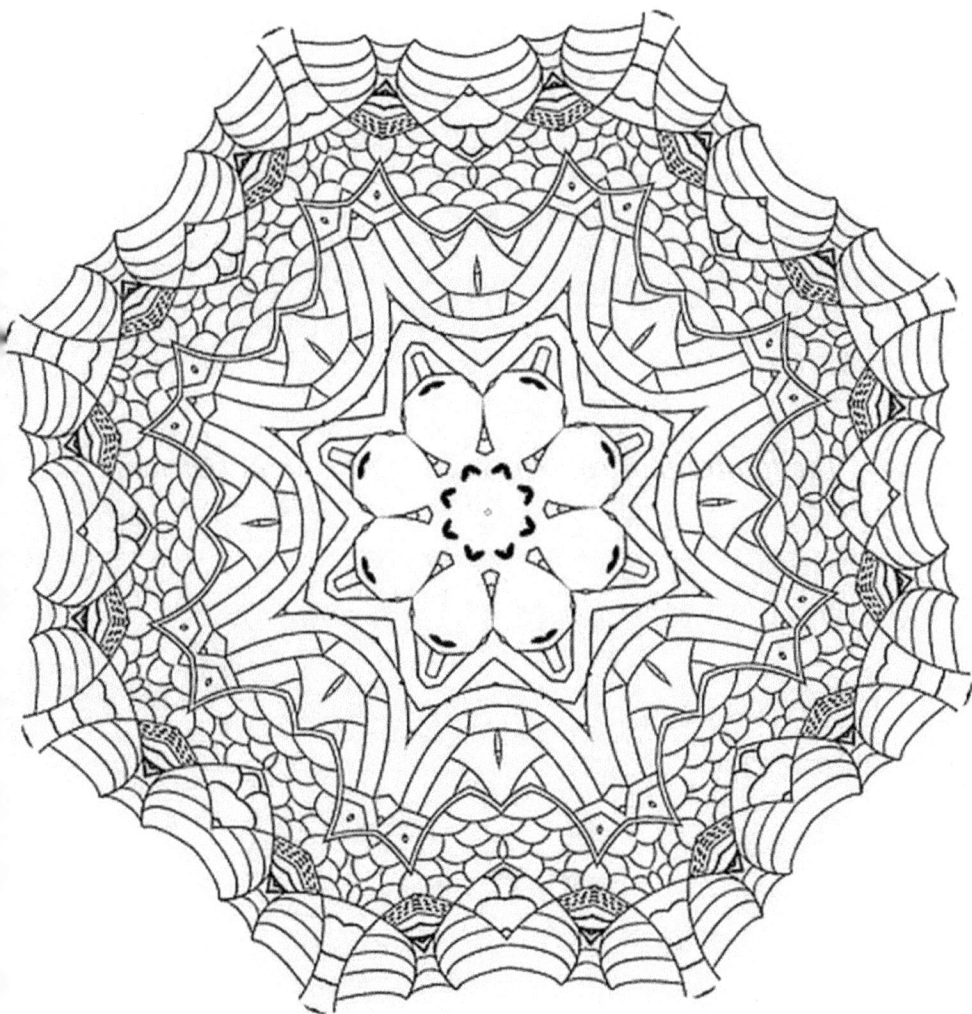

The fountain of content must spring up in the mind.

Johnson

32. PINCER MOVEMENT

The more weakness the more falsehood; strength goes straight.

Richter

33. PSYCHEDELIC MUSHROOMS

The manner of giving shows the character of the giver
more than the gift itself.

Lavater

34. READY FOR TAKE OFF!

Real and solid happiness springs from moderation.

Goethe

35. ROCKET LAUNCH

Do naught to others which, if done to thee, would cause thee pain.

Mahābhārata

36. ROCKIN' ROCKETS

Set about whatever you intend to do; the beginning is half the battle.

Ausonius

37. SHE SELLS SEA SHELLS

There is nothing more beautiful than cheerfulness in an old face.

Richter

38. SHY RABBITS

It is not enough to know; we must apply what we know.

Goethe

39. SLEEPING ANGELS

A jewel preserves its lustre, though trodden in the mud.

Panchatantra

40. SPOTTY SWALLOWS

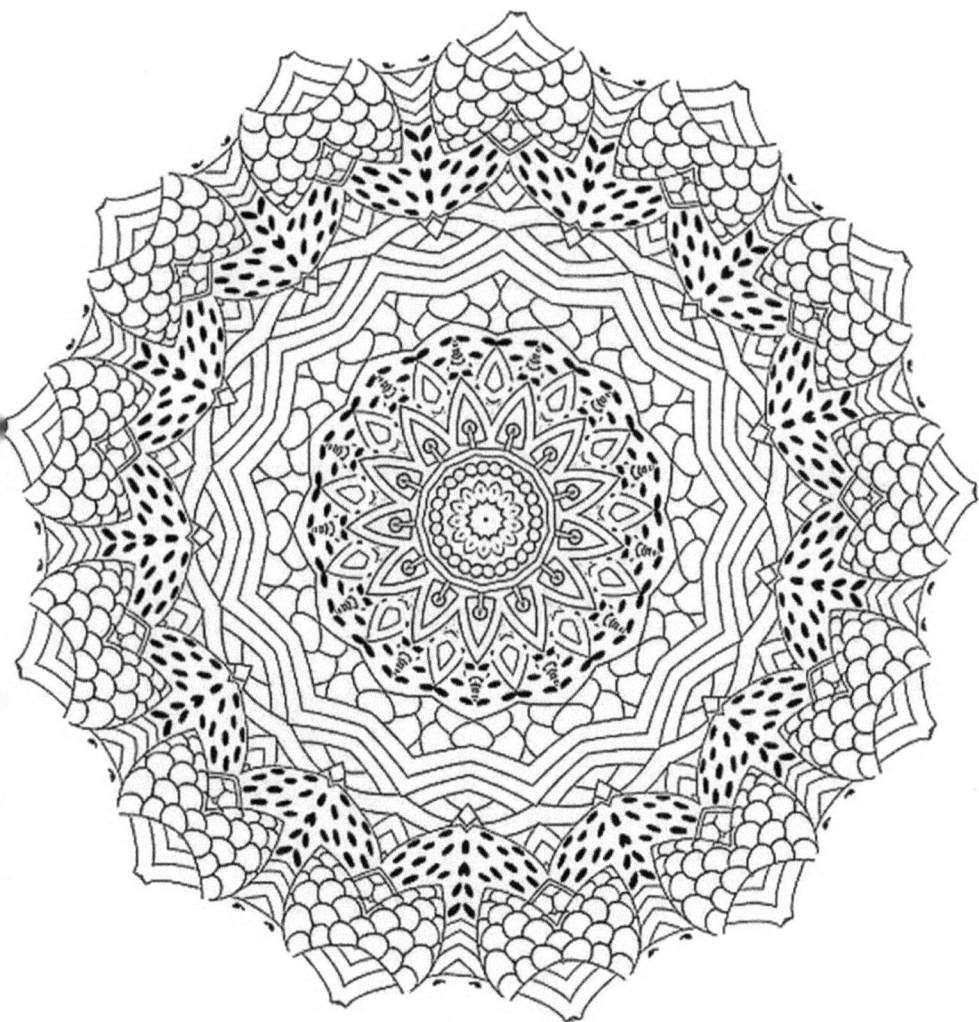

Every gift, though small, is in reality great, if it be given with affection.

Philemon

41. SURPRISE!

Wisdom alone is the true and unalloyed coin for which we ought to exchange all things.

Plato

42. TALKING TERRIERS

If you intend to do a good act, do it quickly.

Ausonius

43. TECHNICOLOR YAWN

A truly great man never puts away the simplicity of a child.

Chinese saying

44. THE BUTTERFLIES' CHRISTMAS

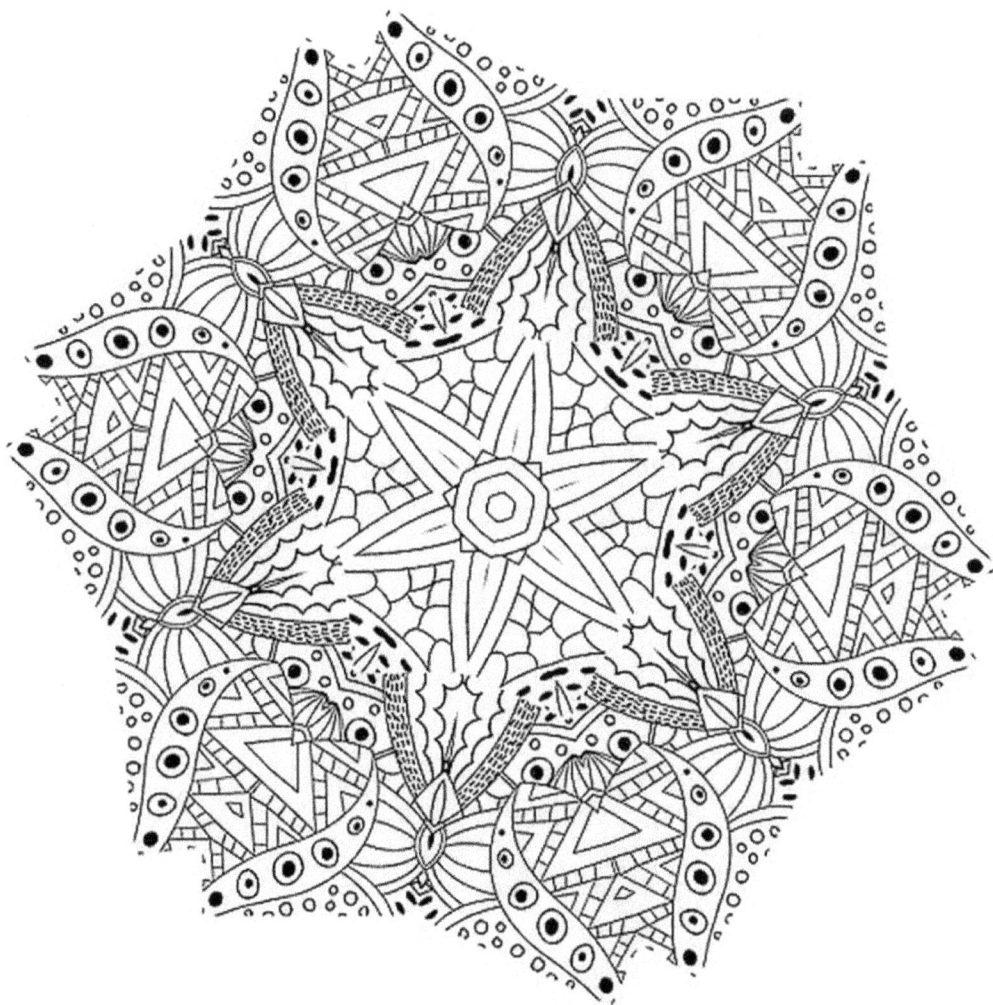

*If you should find your friend in the wrong reprove them
secretly, but in the presence of company praise them.*

Arabic saying

45. TIGER DIVAS

Talents are best nurtured in solitude; character is best formed in the stormy billows of the world.

Goethe

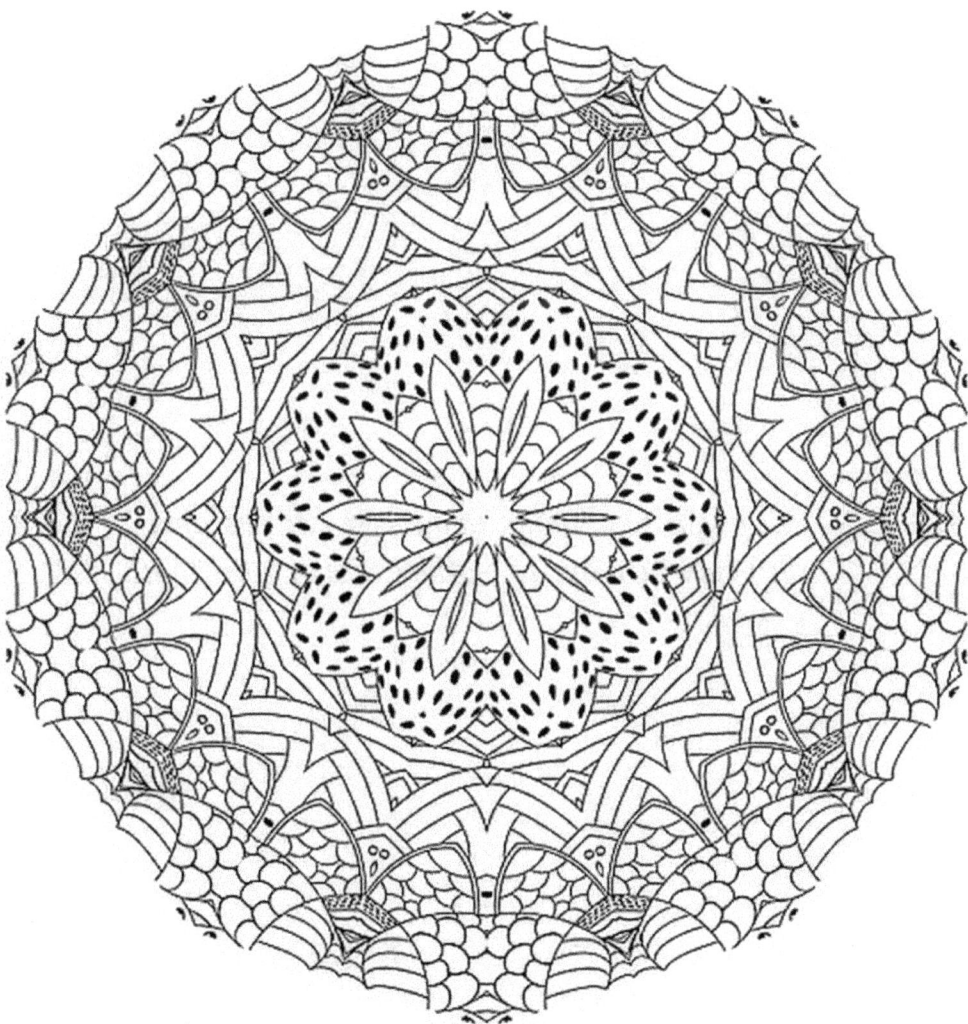

46. TIGER LILY

No one ought to despond in adverse circumstances, for they may turn out to be the cause of good to us.

Menander

47. TOADSTOOL FAIRY RING

As the potter forms what he pleases with soft clay, so a person accomplishes his works by his own act.

Hitopadesa

48. TRAUMATIZED TORTOISES

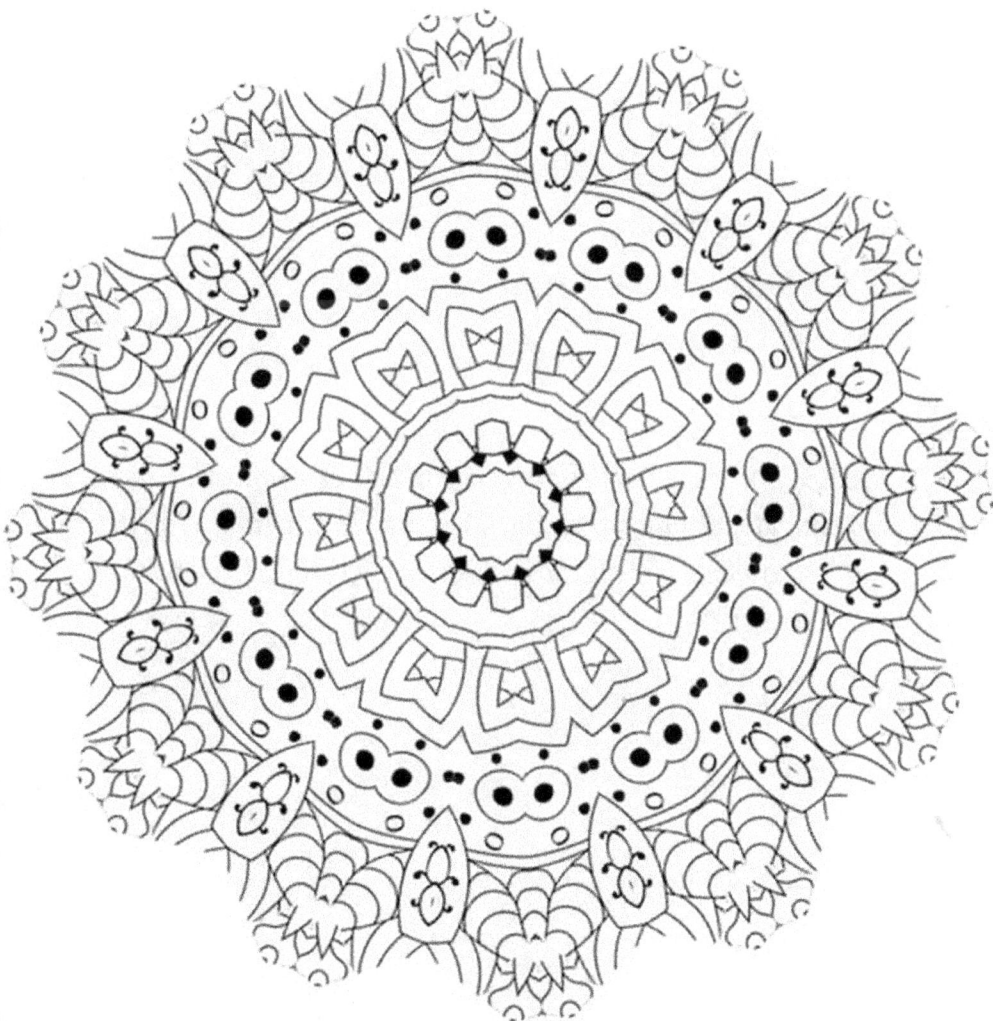

Look not mournfully into the Past. It comes not back again. Wisely improve the Present. It is thine. Go forth to meet the shadowy Future, without fear.

Longfellow

49.TRIBAL TROUBLE

Every person stamps their value on themselves. We are made great or little by our own will.

Schiller

50. VERY INCA

We hope you have enjoyed this book. We'd love to hear from you so why not visit our website: www.dramallamapress.com or write to us at info@dramallamapress.com

Sign up for the Drama Llama Press newsletter for our new releases and get our short problem solving e-book *Solved in a Day* free!

Click here to get started or go to www.dramallamapress/newsletter/

www.ingramcontent.com/pod-product-compliance
Lightning Source LLC
Chambersburg PA
CBHW061752020426
42331CB00006B/1437